Made in United States
North Haven, CT
15 February 2023

32617561R00074